Mark Gould

Poems for the Times on Prevalent Customs and Essential Reforms

Relating Chiefly to Temperance and the Sabbath

Mark Gould

Poems for the Times on Prevalent Customs and Essential Reforms
Relating Chiefly to Temperance and the Sabbath

ISBN/EAN: 9783337296575

Printed in Europe, USA, Canada, Australia, Japan

Cover: Foto ©Thomas Meinert / pixelio.de

More available books at **www.hansebooks.com**

POEMS FOR THE TIMES

— ON —

Prevalent Customs and Essential Reforms

RELATING CHIEFLY TO

TEMPERANCE AND THE SABBATH,

— WITH —

ILLUSTRATIVE STATISTICS AND FACTS.

By Rev. MARK GOULD, A. M.

Author of "Pictures of Zion," "The Land of Rest," Etc.

FLORENCE PUBLISHING CO.
WORCESTER, MASS., AND NEW YORK.
1891.

CONTENTS.

I. THE TEMPERANCE REFORM.

	PAGE.
Reformatory Demands of the Times. Introductory,	5
The Fiery Flood,	9
Conquests of Truth,	12
Freedom Proclaimed,	16
The Angelic Visitant, in seven parts,	18
Missions and the Liquor Traffic,	49
Rise, Sons of Freedom,	51
High License,	53
The Rising Tide,	55
The Captive Released,	57
Seed Sowing,	60
A Temperance Song for Independence Day,	61
The Supreme Reformer,	63
Statistical Notes on the Temperance Reform,	95

1. The Saloon. 2. What Liquor Costs. 3. Crime. 4. Disease. 5. Poverty and Pauperism. 6. Benefits of Prohibition. 7. Prohibition Practicable. 8. Ancient Prohibitory Laws. 9. Missions and Strong Drinks.

CONTENTS.—CONCLUDED.

II. Temperance in Practice.

	PAGE.
Danger of Moderate Drinking,	73
Self-Inflicted Woe,	74
The Murderer and the Vender,	79
Youthful Resolves. Lyrical,	78
Juvenile Ballads,	79
Children Warned. A Lyric,	80
Tobacco and Reform. A Handmaid of Rum,	81
Illustrations in Prose,	83

III. Sabbatic Poems.

	PAGE.
Institution of the Sabbath,	85
The "Queen of Days,"	87
Abolition of the Sabbath,	89
Trampling on the Sabbath,	91
Proofs and Facts Relating to the Sabbath,	93
Tribute to the Memory of Florence Eglantine Gould, and Abbie Rosa Gould,	95

I.—The Temperance Reform.

REFORMATORY DEMANDS OF THE TIMES.

INTRODUCTORY.

We live in grand progressive years,
Though mid conflicting hopes and fears,
   And in a constant strife ;
While great reformers are abroad,
Whose feet have many countries trod ;
Sin whets its sword to conquer God,
   And death opposes life.

A Leader has gone forth in might,
Who arms His servants for the fight
   And gives His Spirit's aid ;
He teaches them what foes to meet,
And in the conflict guides their feet,
Protecting them from sore defeat,
   That they be not afraid.

This Leader, when He came to earth,
And gave the Christian Kingdom birth,
　　To His disciples said,
Think not I came to bring you peace,
To cause all conflicts here to cease.
—Not thus will righteousness increase,
　　Not thus His empire spread.

As He foretold, the conflict came,
Fierce Persecution lit her flame
　　To counteract the Word;
When this to mighty conquest rose,
It met a host of stubborn foes,
Who sought with error to oppose,
　　With torture, fire and sword.

So, in our own more favored days,
When we the Temperance banner raise,
　　And Sabbaths seek to save,
The more we work for such reforms,
The fiercer rage opposing storms:
Yet more the light the world adorns,
　　Though madly tempests rave.

The flowers that in their beauty bloom,
Diffusing wide their sweet perfume,
　　The rain, in shower or storm ;
The river, as it calmly flows,
The wind that swift or gently blows,
The hoary frost and wintry snows,
　　Their purposes perform.

For self alone, do you suppose
The sun with all its radiance glows,
　　And stars their courses keep?
Not for himself alone should man,
Contrive to form a working plan,
But toil for others as he can,
　　And not inactive, sleep.

While God in nature works His will,
His plans stupendous to fulfill
　　Through all the realms of space,
For man He has a mission too,
And special work for him to do,
Of which he needs to have a view
　　That he may fill his place.

To guide the erring, help the weak,
Kind words of admonition speak,
  And use the franchise well;
To train the young in wisdom's way,
That they may never go astray,
Reclaim inebriates if we may,
  All vice and crime expel;

To purify our nation's laws,
And help sustain the Saviour's cause
  In all the lands of earth;
To give the light of gospel day
To those who long in darkness lay;
To warn and teach, to watch and pray
  And show the Saviour's worth.

Such is the work that God requires,
For this the quickened heart aspires,
  This will the life adorn;
The Lord His kingdom is to take,
And all things new He is to make;
He came this work to undertake,
  This glorious Reform.

THE FIERY FLOOD.

Like lava from the mountain side
   Wild sweeps o'er earth a seething tide,
Spreads desolation in its train,
   O'er solid land and heaving main.

This dread volcano never tires,
   But ceaseless are its scathing fires;
The stream augments and wider spreads,
   Till every shore its havoc dreads.

In many places naught remains
   Of gardens fair and fruitful plains,
But lands by barrenness defaced,
   Where desolation's path is traced.

Nor this alone; but buildings neat,
   That smiled along the lovely street,
Whole towns and cities, once so fair,
   Show signs of ruin here and there.

THE FIERY FLOOD.

The tide sweep o'er, and on the State,
   Now brings disloyalty and hate,
Turns law into iniquity,
   And wastes the public treasury.

Where'er the fiery torrent flows,
   It brings a train of want and woes,
While peaceful harmony departs
   From homes where once were cheerful hearts.

See men, in God's own image made,
   Turned into brutes, in ditches laid,
Or reeling homewards to their gates,
   To meet their sad, despairing mates.

Hear you the loud, distressful cry,
   That comes from hungry children nigh,
For daily bread, for clothes to wear,
   For needed, kind, paternal care?

See reason driven from its throne,
   While greed and passion rule alone,
And crimes of every name and grade
   Become the victim's chosen trade.

THE FIERY FLOOD.

Thus swept upon the deadly tide,
   How long can man himself abide?
How soon he fills a drunkard's grave,
   Though God and neighbors seek to save!

Ye fires of appetite that burn,
   And all restraints of reason spurn,
We long have sought to roll you back,
   And renovate your wasted track.

The struggle may be fierce and long,
   Before we raise the victors song;
But He who stilled the raging sea,
   For such a work must equal be.

The temperance banner, now unfurled,
   E'er long shall float o'er all the world,
For He before our army goes,
   Who ne'er defeat or failure knows.

CONQUESTS OF TRUTH.

Swifter than the winds that blow,
   Mightier than the earthquake's throw,
Sharper than a two-edge sword
   Is the everlasting word.

Jewish rulers, priest and scribe
   All in vain the truth deride ;
Pagans, armed with power arise,
   Rome her allied forces tries.

See the artful Julian
   Use the utmost powers he can,
To exterminate the word,
   That it may no more be heard.

Hear him, when about to die,
   To his failure testify,
Conquered own himself to be
   By the Man of Galilee.

Papal. Moslem powers, in vain
   Make the like attempts again,
Using weapons, tortures, fire,
   To accomplish their desire.

Wickliff, Tyndale, Luther rose,
   All such efforts to oppose;
Multiplied the word divine,
   Caused the light of truth to shine.

Satan then resolved to be
   Backed by infidelity;
France most impiously decreed
   That there is no God indeed.

Still the truth held on its way,
   Turning darkness into day;
Widely is it now diffused,
   Howsoever much abused.

Errors flee like mists of morn,
   Sciences the world adorn,
Truth and grace go forth to reign
   O'er the spacious earth and main.

Plies the Demon still his arts,
    Scatters wide his fiery darts,
Vile intoxicants employs,
    Soul and body both destroys.

Everywhere in marts of trade
    Tempting flagons are displayed;
Those of every class and age
    Quaff the poisonous beverage.

Low inebriates are found
    Staggering and lounging round;
Crime and beggary and woe
    O'er the land in torrents flow.

Where is truth? It is not dead,
    See it boldly raise its head;
Pulpit, press, societies
    On the scene like magic rise.

Now the enemy retreats,
    Hides himself in meaner streets;
Truth advances armed with power,
    For it is its conquering hour.

Let the plastic minds of youth,
    Humbly yield to Gospel truth ;
Then the tempting power of rum
    Surely shall not overcome.

Truth the fallen can restore,
    To be abject slaves no more ;
Can restrain the appetite,
    Guiding, moulding man aright.

Gog and Magog need not try
    God almighty to defy ;
Truth shall everywhere prevail,
    And its powers shall never fail.

Great the conquests it has gained,
    Greater still shall be obtained ;
Onward then to victory,
    Ye who would full triumph see.

Wield the sword of truth with might,
    Battle bravely for the right ;
Trusting in the Lord most high,
    Never falter, faint or fly.

FREEDOM PROCLAIMED.

There comes a voice from Calvary,
    Proclaiming glorious liberty,
To those who long were captives bound,
    For whom a ransom has been found.

'Tis blood that precious freedom gives,
    Once shed by Him who risen lives;
Its virtues still the Father owns,
    For all believers it atones.

No might of warriors now we need,
    No other advocate to plead;
The Gospel heralds wide proclaim
    Redemption through a Saviour's name.

The message flies around the world,
    And Freedom's banner is unfurled;
Fast swells the kingdom of the free,
    Wide rings the shout of liberty.

But still the prince of darkness reigns
   O'er millions, held in slavish chains;
The call to freedom kindly made,
   By multitudes is not obeyed.

Vast numbers have not even heard
   That freedom is by Christ conferred;
While many more have not believed
   The gracious message, when received.

Send forth thy Word, great Lord of light,
   Attended by the Spirit's might;
Till every kindred, tribe and State,
   Emancipation celebrate.

Spread, kingdom of the noble free,
   From land to land, from sea to sea;
Thy children, one by one, shall rise
   To endless freedom in the skies.

THE ANGELIC VISITANT.

I.

Imagination's wildly soaring wing,
From worlds remote can useful lessons bring,
Make darkened truth in brighter colors shine,
So well accomplished in the word divine.
Methought, from realms beyond the vaulted sky,
Where dwells the Lord in majesty most high,
On pinions swift an angel downward flew,
And soon the earth spread out before his view.
What was the object of his advent strange?
What led him from his home so far to range?
Was he inspired by curiosity,
To swim the seas of space, new things to see,
And learn what works of genus, art and skill,
Adorn the land, and towns and cities fill?
Or would he nature's wondrous works behold,
As wrought by God, with beauties manifold,
And learn what wonders, the wide world around,

To gratify and teach, were to be found?
A nobler object wakes his fond desires,
A higher aim his mind and heart inspires.

 Analogy had well convinced his mind,
That he on earth intelligence would find
In those, whom He who rules the world He made,
Had formed; to ascertain their state and grade
In that great scale, which in its height extends
To angels ministrant, and which descends
To lowest forms that tenant air and earth,
Or in the spacious waters have their birth;
To learn their character, conditions, laws,
Their virtues, vices, and of these the cause;
Such were the themes that occupied his thought,
And such the knowledge which he sagely sought;
As Howard on his godlike errand bent
Through climes remote and hostile regions went,
In dungeons drear to raise the drooping heart,
Relief, advice and comfort to impart.

 First on a verdant spot he chanced to rest,
And there he cast his view from east to west,
To north and south: resplendent was the view,
Of earth, in vernal robes arrayed; the dew

Of morning glistened in the playful beams,
On beauteous plants and flowers and flowing streams;
The gentle, bleating flocks, the lowing herds,
Sonorous notes of gay aerial birds,
The zephyrs, whispering through gigantic trees,
The din of business, and the hum of bees
He heard, while 'neath his feet sprang herbage green,
And wide on every hand were to be seen
Impressive marks of plenty, wealth and joy,
Which nothing had invaded to destroy.
The hand of man had changed fair nature's face,
For heaven born industry had left a trace
On every spot; and therefore everywhere,
Order and beauty, that united pair,
Appeared, the fruit of human toil and skill,
The eye to charm, the heart with pleasure fill.
Some pleasant buildings he espied, whose forms
Appeared well fitted to dispel the storms,
And shield from rude extremes of heat and cold,
The living beings they were made to hold.

 When gladly toward a well built residence
He turned his quickened steps, intelligence
Was seen inscribed on every thing around,

For, thrift without, and health within were found,
He saw the inmates gathered round the board,
Profuse with all that plenty could afford.
Not there was seen the tempting cup whence flowed
Destructive poison; healthful water flowed,
Which God, the everlasting Father brewed,
And far and wide upon the earth has strewed, .
Transparent as the glassy mirror's face,
And harmless as a messenger of grace.
The host received him with a welcome kind,
Nor questioned what the stranger guest designed;
A hospitable smile his visage wore,
And signs of noble dignity he bore;
Large stores of useful knowledge he possessed,
To guide the young, and comfort the distressed.
A gentle partner joined with him to share
The common blessing and the common care:
Their children, objects of parental love,
Most precious gifts of Him who reigns above,
Cheerful and blooming with the flush of health
And joyful in the plentitude of wealth,
Appeared like flowers in beauteous colors dressed,
And with the genial rays of morning blest

The breakfast o'er, the host with a solemn look,
Down from the burdened shelf a comely volume took.
The family, in mute, attentive mood,
Were seated round him, like a modest brood;
On food that fills the hungry soul they fed,
And drank of living fountains while he read.
It was a book that pointed out to man
His state and duties, and revealed the plan,
The best that heavenly wisdom could conceive,
To save from ruin, and the fall retrieve.
It gave a record of those wondrous deeds,
By Him performed from whom all good proceeds.
A portion read, he knelt in fervent prayer,
Devoutly owning God's paternal care;
His own, and others' sinfulness deplored,
And pardon sought of Him whom he adored,
For kindred, neighbors, all mankind he prayed,
That by them all the Lord might be obeyed.
He closed his orison, and then in songs
They honor Him to whom all praise belongs.

The service ended, to their work they went,
With grateful hearts, and free from discontent;
In healthful industry the day was past,

THE ANGELIC VISITANT.

And when the shades of evening gathered fast;
When stars came forth to greet returning night,
And moon dffused her soft and silvery light,
The happy group was found where it had been,
Again to pray and tune the grateful hymn.

II.

When morn awoke and widely flung its light
O'er smiling earth, and made creation bright,
The guest prepared to leave the peaceful dome
Untended on his pilgrimage to roam.
While passing through some glades of leafy trees,
Whose branches sported in the passing breeze,
He mused upon the scenes of yesterday,
And fell into a mute soliloquy:
Is this a picture true of man's whole race,
And such his happy state in every place?
Then may he boast of origin devine,
Nor should he ever murmnr or repine.
His state is one of heartfelt happiness,
And demonstrates that on the earth true bliss
Is found, which feeble, mortal man may know
And make his own; for what could God bestow

On beings dwelling in this sunlit sphere,
Which has not been profusely lavished here?
  While thoughts like these employed his pensive mind,
At once a sudden, sad surprise to find
The prospect changed, ran through his very frame;
The blameless earth no more appeared the same;
But when he cast his eyes attentive round,
He naught but marks of desolation found.
What curse was here? O! what foul blast of death
Has swept earth's bosom; what dark demon's breath
Has spread his poison here? The cause is not
That showers and breezes were denied this spot;
'Tis not that savage beasts, or birds of prey
The products of the earth have snatched away;
'Tis not that yon resplendent sun refused
To shed his rays, and has not warmth infused;
Nor yet because the teeming soil declined
To yield productions of a useful kind.
The plants around in rich luxuriance rise,
 And flowers innoxious with the noxious vies;
Weeds, tall and rank, support the rising blade,
Prevent its growth and cause it soon to fade;
The bristling thistle raised its head in pride,

THE ANGELIC VISITANT.

With piercing thorns and briers at its side;
Here the rough time-worn hedge lay prostrate all,
And there it seemed just tottering to its fall;
The herd had made a pasture of the field,
And swine awaited what the glebe might yield.
Near by a brown and shattered building rose,
Which well he judged some inmates to enclose.

  As near he drew and carefully surveyed,
The windows here their broken glass displayed,
And there, were filled with rags or crockery,
Which gave to our astonished guest a view
Of scenes, as wonderful as they were new.
A family sat round the scanty board,
Which seemed to say, no more could we afford.
The children were in tattered garments clad,
Their actions rude, their countenances sad.

  The host gave cool reception to his guest,
For selfish feelings filled his callous breast,
Not to his table was that guest received,
Or asked what wants he had to be relieved;
And when to quit his meal the father rose,
No prayer was raised to Him who good bestows,
No blessing sought, no portion of God's word

Was read, no song of grateful praise was heard.
  The wife and children to their labor went,
But not the husband; who was not content
To spend his time in honest industry,
Or in the bosom of his family.
He chose to go, the stranger knew not where;
To follow and observe was now his care.
He wished to learn, from what his eyes had seen,
Why such wide difference was found between
These neighboring spots; fain would he learn
What baneful scourge, what foe to man could turn
A family, where love and happiness
Should ever dwell, and every member bless,
To one of discord, want and misery,
Which there the visitor was pained to see
Impressed on every form of human shape.
The wanderer from home began to prate,
As on they passed, and soon betrayed a mind
Devoid of sense, to truth and reason blind.

III.

  While they in converse traveled on their way,
A pleasant prospect soon before them lay;

From birds of plumage matin songs awoke,
And sweetest lays from groves of beauty broke,
Bright flowers through all the air their odors shed,
And from the stranger's heart dejection fled.
At once his eyes with heightened pleasure rest
On rich plantations, in green verdure dressed;
While stately houses, lining all the street,
In beauteous colors smiled 'mid arbors neat.

As on they travelled soon a village spire
Burst on his vision; then did he inquire
Of his companion, what great building there
Towered up and glistened in the morning air.
When told that there large congregations meet
To hear God's word and worship at His feet,
The thought that God was honored he should find,
Now burst at once upon the stranger's mind.

A street they entered, lined on either side
With houses neat, of villagers the pride;
But here and there a single mansion stood,
Whose aspect and condition were not good.
The guide conducting, soon they leave the street,
And enter where a frightful host they meet,
Whose face the aspect of a savages wore,

Whose eyes the lustre of a demon bore.
Around him stood a group much like himself,
Who talked of pleasure, appetite and pelf,
Now on professing Christians would they rail,
And now with oaths profane their neighbors hail.
They cursed the day when temperance had its birth
And Spirits called best products of the earth;
Some would the semblance of a reason give
For what they said; some thought the temperate should live,
For mercy's sake, and yet be punished well,
Since they against man's freedom dared rebel.
Amazement chilled the stranger's inmost heart,
As gazing on the scene he stood apart.

  To tell the thoughts that through his bosom ran,
While there he mused upon the state of man,
The effort would be vain: soon greet his view,
Some objects strange to him as they were new.
Upon the counter stood tall long necked things,
And each beside, a pair of glasses twines.
Man after man, approaching filled his glass,
Which round to others they would quickly pass.
What was within? There must the secret be,
To all the former mysteries the key.

It tempting seemed, for sparkling was its hue,
And those who took it always drank it too.
No more about its nature could he glean,
Than what from its effects was to be seen;
These were not absent, plain before his eyes,
They were developed, quit of all disguise.

   Already some are staggering round the room,
And one lay prostrate like a helpless broom;
The liquid to their cheeks a glow imparts,
And from their eyes a fiendlike lustre darts.
The stranger reads upon the bottles drained,
The titles of the matter they contained;
He then, in firm, but gentle words addressed,
The heartless dealer, singled from the rest;
O man of earth, in traffic dire you deal,
And have you not a heart this truth to feel?
Then go with me to visit yonder farm,
And then you cannot say, it is no harm.
Will you pretend quite innocent to be,
In causing drunkenness and misery?
The whiskey, rum and brandy which you sell,
Must be the potions and the drugs of hell.
Desist, desist, away the poison fling,

Or on your head it must dire vengence bring.
Does justice sleep? If so it soon will wake,
And on yourself will all its thunders break ;
Already to my ears the acts have come
By those, your customers, in frenzy done;
You furnish weapons for the murderous deed,
The hearts of countless worthy widows bleed
For hopes extinguished by such liquid fires,
And children weep for loved but ruined sires.
In haste reverse your course, for know,
There is a God who looks on man below,
You cannot 'scape His ire ; if men and laws
Should fail to plead the injured orphan's cause,
Though serpent-like the harmless you beguile
And wash your hands as innocent the while,
Thus 'twill not always be ; His wrath will wake,
And on the two-edged sword of vengence take.

 But senseless as a statue stood the man,
No soft emotion through his bosom ran ;
To this advice rude answer he returned,
And both the counsellor and counsel spurned.
Shall I of food my family deprive,
And give to others all the chance to thrive?

Both law and custom give the right to me
To use in this free land my liberty;
Each year a license to make sales I buy,
And yet this right and freedom you deny.

  The stranger answered; right to do the wrong
Can not by any means to man belong;
All have full liberty the *right* to do,
But those their freedom lose who *wrong* pursue;
As harmless birds can freely range the air,
While those that mischief seek provoke the snare;
Your business, which you deem of great avail,
May ruin on yourself and sons entail;
Though human law your traffic legalize,
There reigns a higher Ruler in the skies,
Whose laws prohibit every evil deed,
And bid all men there neighbors weal to heed;
Those who His righteous mandates disregard,
Will find the way of the transgressor hard,
As rebel angels hastily were driven
To *dreary realms? far from there native heaven.*

IV.

The missionary on his journey went,

On gaining information still intent;
And soon his eyes observant saw a place
Which brought upon the neighborhood disgrace.
He learned through odors which from windows came,
That liquors there were made, of various name.
Here piles of grain the spacious chamber strew,
There massive hogsheads meet his wondering view,
And barrels hiding unseen foes within,
Here rows of whiskey, there ensnaring gin.
 He sought the office, and with thoughts oppressed.
The mute distiller with these words addressed:
O man of earth, you certainly must know,
That here you manufacture human woe!
Why turn the wholesome products of the field
To instruments which death and sorrow yield?
Why pain, disease and wretchedness distil
From what man's heart with healthful joy should fill?
If millions you should gain, 'twill not repay
For judgments sore which will not long delay;
At length will conscience from its slumber wake,
And then the sword of vengeance God will take.
 The sharp retort is given: Pray why should you
Condemn as infamous what here I do?

Do not mechanics use what I produce,
And druggists turn it to a healthful use?
If other classes in their freedom choose
What I produce as beverage to use,
Must I be censured for their foolishness,
And charged with manufacturing distress!
   But while such earnest colloquy they hold,
A pamphlet from the shelf a story told,
Which opened more the missionary's eyes,
And shocked his feelings with a fresh surprise.
It taught the secret, wicked chemistry
Of mixing drugs with liquors skilfully.
On seeing this the stranger still proceeds,
To charge the man with his inhuman deeds:
'Tis not enough one poison to employ,
You many mix, more quickly to destroy;
You sell a compound, treacherous and vile,
And this the slaves of appetite beguile.
The guilty hearer ventured no reply;
He knew it vain the charges to deny;
Although his conscience loudly said, repent,
Persistent in his wicked path he went.
   Away the missionary turned his feet,

And traveled onward through a lonely street :
The distant city, in proud beauty dressed,
Awakened new desires within his breast,
Some leading speakers he desired to hear,
And note what indications might appear
Of vice or virtue; ascertain the cause
Why crimes were not restrained, what kind of laws
Were found upon the legal statute book,
And what positions legislators took.
As through frequented streets he passed along,
He heard inebriates chantng senseless song :
And blazing o'er shopkeepers doors appear
The signs which told, We sell destruction here.
He sees the victims hasten to the snare,
And make themselves intoxicated there ;
As when the fishers with their baits entice,
And snatch the foolish eaters in a trice.

When shades of evening round the stranger fell,
He heard, not far, a loud resounding bell,
And rightly guessed, from what he heard and saw,
That 'twas designed the people there to draw:
Within the building where was heard the sound,
A waiting congregation large he found ;

The speaker entering soon discourse began,
And thus the theme of his oration ran.

  He showed how alcohol had widely reigned,
And over every class had triumph gained,
When early in the present century
The ranks of temperance started gloriously;
What enemies they met, what conquests won,
While battling they together moved as one,
And sought with energy on every hand
To drive the cruel monster from the land;
But when division ran throughout the host,
And many of new schemes began to boast,
When none were wanted publicly to speak,
But those who late had been among the weak,
Who oft their subject poorly understood,
And sometimes vilified the truly good,
Then did the wheels of temperance slowly move.
And what was wisdom thought, did folly prove;
Destruction greater impetus obtained,
And larger spoils and influence it gained;
While States and Towns still generally sold
Their licenses to ruin young and old.

  Then in the East a Star of promise rose,

In laws designed such madness to oppose;
Although beginning in the State of Maine,
They soon attention through the country gain,
And find adoption in some other States,
So that Reform extensive progress makes.
But soon its wheels receive impediment,
When Parties, on ascendency intent,
Esteemed the measure politic and wise,
To make of Prohibition sacrifice.
'Twas passing strange that they no evil saw,
In framing rank iniquity by law.
E'en where good laws already had been made,
Of exrcuting them some were afraid.

When great the mischief which had thus been done,
Some Western women to the rescue come;
Who wield the instrument of mighty prayer,
And great the victories accomplished there.
As on the car of Reformation moves,
It sometimes runs through unaccustomed grooves,
And by degrees the truth becomes impressed,
That Gospel means and forces are the best;
And that by help divine in mercy given,
Are chains of Appetite most surely riven.

THE ANGELIC VISITANT.

The speaker closing, loud was the applause,
Which showed a general interest in the cause;
Though here and there was dissonance expressed,
While truth had been with eloquence expressed.
The stranger listened with attentive ears,
And found within his breast both hopes and fears.

V.

Again he enters on the public way,
A visit to the Capitol to pay:
The spacious State-house shortly greets his eyes,
Towards which successive steps of granite rise;
The Legislative Halls within were great,
And there were gathered men from all the State;
Some looked like those ordained of heaven to rule,
And others more prepared to play the fool.
At length one moved, that, for the public weal
The well known License Law they should repeal,
And from the Statute Book remove disgrace.
The motion seconded, at once commenced
Some arguments against, and in defence.

One boldly plead, 'Tis not Democracy
To take from business men their liberty:
He thought his party never would consent

To bring upon its friends such punishment.
Another said that Taverns would be closed,
If thus their fattest traffic was opposed;
That this the traveling public would alarm,
And bring on certain classes needless harm.
He further claimed that such a course would soon
Close every handy dram shop and saloon,
And thus drive many from their loved employ,
Their gains and cherished prospects to destroy.

Then one arose, the motion to defend,
And strongly for its passage to contend.
He said: If your Democracy requires
To multiply and foster liquid fires,
That desolation spread o'er all the land,
And leave their trail of woe on every hand,
Shall such Democracy be understood
By men of sense the most consummate good?
Democracy the peoples good should seek,
And from undue temptation guard the weak,
And why should any one have liberty
To hoard up wealth by others misery?
If taverns live on rum, who can deny
'Tis best and fittest that they quickly die?

And as for all your dram shops and saloons,
They chiefly serve inebriate poltroons.
There followed this a shout of loud applause
From those who stood for good and wholesome laws;
While sighs and hisses showed the sharp dissent
Of many on defense of wrong intent.

  Then quickly from his seat another rose.
The pending motion sternly to oppose;
Republican, indeed he claimed to be,
Who sought his party from such harm to free.
The argument he first essayed to use,
Was chosen that the wrong he might excuse:
It was that those enactments must be vain,
Which those who make them cannot well sustain;
That violated laws upon the statute book,
Respect from law and legislation took.
Another argument he further pleads,
That License meets the people's public needs:
He shows how greatly and how readily
It helps to fill the hungry treasury;
That license fees were but a tax, he claimed,
And should not, therefore, license fees be named;
That prohibition laws are understood,

To grant *some* licences for public good.
He said that License Laws are guarded well,
Since men of good repute have right to sell.
   Such were the tunes, repeated o'er and o'er,
The tongues of many other speakers bore.
But this aroused the friends of temperance brave,
And sharp were answers which their speakers gave.
One gravely asked if, in the laws divine,
Of License they could see a single sign,
And drew from thence the inference complete,
That this was not for man made statutes meet.
Does God, he said, from giving laws refrain,
Because the lawless make them partly vain?
Who will pretend that, for the public weal,
'Tis right to license men to rob and steal,
And other crimes commit of blackest dye,
Because some men authority defy?
If eager crows will prey upon the grain,
And render many wise precautions vain,
Shall farmers give to them admission free,
Their crops to devastate with greed and glee?
Laws for the lawless surely should be made,
Though by them they be often disobeyed:
A law enacted, be it understood,

Has its own proper influence, bad or good;
And ne'er have license laws themselves been found,
Enforced completely all the country round.
If license fees a tax you choose to call,
It surely makes no difference at all;
But very different the licenses
For beverage, and for wholesome purposes.

VI.

Anon another orator proceeds
To meet the argument from public needs,
Some stubborn facts and principles to state,
And thus to close the notable debate.
Your plea for revenue at first looks fair,
But tested, vanishes in empty air;
For greater loss the treasury sustains,
Than e'er by fees for license it obtains;
All observation plainly proves such laws,
Of crime and poverty a fruitful cause;
And what to us the profit, after all,
In robbing Peter and thus paying Paul?

But if our thousands we obtained by rum,
It would not pay for half the mischief done,

In character destroyed and blasted hopes,
In influence that drunkenness promotes,
In placing baits to catch unwary youth,
And turning manhood from the path of truth ;
In filling jails and prisons through the land,
And multiplying crimes on every hand.
To license crime is but to violate
The principles that underlie the State,
And to the crime itself a share to lend ;
For what we license we of course defend.
No law, indeed, will e'er enforce itself,
When laid as a dead letter on the shelf.
A true enforcement how can we expect,
If proper means and efforts we neglect?
The public officers we place in power,
Should be prepared for duties of the hour.

If license best promotes the temperance cause,
Why do inebriates all oppose the laws
Which prohibitionists are wont to choose,
And vote to license what they wish to use?
Some say that prohibition always fails,
And that intemperance with it more prevails.
Let Iowa, with Maine and Kansas speak,

To prove such exparte pleading false and weak.
When congress-men, disgrace to do away,
Delirium Tremens call malaria
Their false pretense, if rightly understood,
Resembles that which labels License good.
Wild beasts by force from mischief you restrain;
Man's freedom to do mischief you maintain.
As well assassins seek to regulate
With partial licenses by laws of state,
As seek to regulate by licenses
Men bent for gain on such foul practices.

But if our move persistent you oppose,
Two other motions I would here propose;
To make our legislation so agree,
That it shall work with perfect harmony.
One is that by a license we permit
Some men all crimes for money to commit;
And thus to revenue abundance add,
To make the covetous and wicked glad.

Another statute, it appears to me,
Would with the license law consistient be;
Would make its operation far more just,
And show results more worthy of our trust:

Let those who make and those who sell, each one,
Be held responsible for mischief done;
Let each one suffer just as much himself,
As he has brought on others for sheer pelf;
On those who ruin bring let ruin fall,
And thus let justice fit be done to all.

VII.

   The chairman now, with compliments profuse,
Proceeds the visitant to introduce.
An orator like him man seldom sees;
Not Cicero, far famed Demosthenes,
Pitt, Sheridan, or Webster, in their prime,
Spake words more wise, more weighty, or sublime.
The substance let me give of what he spake,
That mortal sons of earth may lessons take.
From whence he came he told, and what the cause.
How great his interest in their subject was;
He spoke of what he late had seen and heard
By which his deep emotion had been stirred.

   He said: Wild beasts and serpents may abound on earth,
And dangerous scorpions have here their birth,
But still, from what mine eyes have seen, I know,

That man has not a more destructive foe
Than alcohol; its devastations great
May well engage attention from the State.
If hostile armies should your shores invade,
To plunder and destroy by fire and raid,
Would not officials who should not oppose,
Be justly ranked among their country's foes?
To what makes havoc will you freedom give,
That by the wreck and ruin some may live?
The foe his tens of thousands yearly slays,
And on the hopes and peace of millions preys.
If riches you should gain by vending rum,
Such riches, sure, moth-eaten would become.

A righteous Ruler o'er all worlds bears sway,
Whose word makes certain that He will repay:
If rebel angels from their seats were driven,
Excluded from the precincts of their native heaven,
Can those expect that blest abode to gain,
Who practice evil, and God's laws disdain?
His everlasting word pronounces woe,
On such as give the tempting cup, you know;
While woe awaits the drinker of the cup,
Such woe as, drinking, he cannot drink up;

For as he drinks his appetite grows still,
And woes from liquor constantly distil.
Shall buyers, sellers, licensers, combine
To countenance a most outrageous crime?
Your world abounds in blessings from above,
The tokens of divine, eternal love;
But while the gospel all this love declares,
The arch apostate angel spreads his snares.
Shall Christ, or Demon have from you support?
Of other's ruin will you make a sport?
To service every influence should be pressed,
The evils of intemperance to arrest,
That happiness o'er all the earth may spread,
And all humanity lift up its head.

   If license in one place 'tis right to give
To those who would upon the traffic live,
'Tis right in all; and plainly you can see,
If larger places give such liberty,
By all who live in smaller places round,
Can liquor in their marts of trade be found.
The states, not cities, should the trade control,
For what affects a part, affects the whole;
While central towns the fiery liquid sell,

Beyond them will the evil surely swell,
And there can those in regions round acquire
That which their morbid appetites desire.
Those places prohibition most must need,
Which most the longings for foul drinks do feed:
The friends of order in a State, 'tis plain,
Should join, the entire traffic to restrain;
The Legislature therefore is the place
To save the people from the deep disgrace.

   Let churches, parties, all alike combine,
And licenses to final death consign;
From statute books remove the dismal stain,
Before to visit earth I come again,
That here intemperance may quickly cease,
And virtue, love and happiness increase,
That God may here be honored, man be blest,
And earth in beauty and abundance dressed.

   As Enoch and Elijah grandly rode
On wheels of fire up to their high abode,
From earth on angel pinions now he rose;
Swift through the realms etherial he goes,
To that celestial clime of beauty, where
The holy Three in One, and spirits are:

To those around the throne report he makes,
And lively interest he there awakes.
The great apostles, prophets, martyrs, all,
With seraphs holy, and arch-angels tall,
Give close attention to the fearful strife,
Which on the earth is waged 'twixt death and life:
They see how still the prince of darkness tries
To ruin man, and heaven's great King defies;
They mark the progress which the gospel makes,
And with what speed the Lord His kingdom takes;
Each victory God's people here can boast,
Sends joy and praise through all the heavenly host.

  Think not to hear all that the angel said.
More than to hear one risen from the dead;
Not till the home of spirits we attain,
Shall we with joy such information gain.
If this long dream shall benefit impart,
And help the temperance cause, 'twill cheer my heart.
Let all with ceaseless zeal its progress aid,
That thus the sweeping torrent may be stayed.
Though dreams from multitude of thoughts arise,
Yet happy he who by them is made wise.

MISSIONS AND THE LIQUOR TRAFFIC.

We send the gospel o'er the seas,
   With messengers of heavenly grace;
'Tis in this way the Lord decrees
   To save believers of our race;
We for companions Liquid Poisons send,
   That to debasement and perdition tend.

From our own country thus proceed
   The healing balm, the spring of joy,
The fount of woe, the fruit of greed,
   Man's dreadful foe, the world's alloy;
As if upon the same productive tree,
   Both sweet and bitter fruitage we should see.

How shall we Africa restore
   From direful slavery, sin and woe,
If, while we send the gospel o'er,
   We cause the streams of death to flow;
And spread o'er Ethiopia's plains and hills
   The desolating products of our stills?

MISSIONS AND THE LIQUOR TRAFFIC.

Shall we make darker what is dark,
    And viler what we now deem vile?
In such crusade shall we embark,
    Our hands and record to defile?
On Africa for gain one woe we brought,
    And shall another fearful one be sought?

Was it for this that Moffat went,
    That Livingston such lonely years
Mid wilds unknown, untraversed, spent,
    Enduring hunger, toils and fears;
And Stanley showed himself so bold,
    Whose wondrous story need not here be told?

Ye who that Continent would gain,
    To bud and blossom as the rose,
That there in triumph Christ may reign,
    Take heed the deadly fount to close;
And send not with the messengers of life,
    The fiery liquid, with destruction rife.

RISE, SONS OF FREEDOM.

Comes a piteous cry of anguish
  From the homes on hill and vale,
Where the hearts of matrons languish,
  Where the hopes of children fail,
And a wild devouring demon leaves·
            his dark and deadly trail.

From each hamlet, town and city
  O'er this wide extended land,
Rises up the voice of pity
  For the woes on every hand
Which relief, efficient, speedy,
            most assuredly demand.

Lo, a slavery worse than Afric,
  Binds its countless victims still,
Men pursue a deadly traffic
  With the products of the Still;
Wives and children weep in sadness,
            fathers graves and prisons fill.

See the mobs and tumults raging,
    Wielding flames and dynamite,
Lawless anarchists engaging
    In mad conflict with the right;
While a rum incited rabble
        urges onward to the fight,

Now demands our high endeavor,
    Utmost energy and skill,
Conflict with a foe which ever
    Seeks to triumph o'er the will,
And the land with crime and bloodshed,
        poverty and woe to fill!

Ye, whose fathers broke the shackles,
    Forged in England's lordly court;
Ye who freed there million chattels,
    Made of tyranny the sport,
Now make valient fight for freedom,
        and secure a proud report.

HIGH LICENSE.

Come, let us put a higher price
   On vending what produces vice,
Say some who would be wise;
   Let rivulets to rivers turn,
That more from selling we may earn,
   They plausably advise.

But shall we make respectable
   What is with infamy so full,
And grant monopoly
   To those who hold an honored place,
And thus diminish the disgrace
   Of great iniquity!

Whate'er the license, high or low,
   Alike its evil and its woe,
From principle afar;
   It gives to crime a speciousness,
And, covering the wickedness,
   Yokes mammon to its car.

HIGH LICENSE.

Whatever people say or think,
  Woe follows those who give strong drink;
Then is it wrong to give
  The license, be it low or high,
  By which are thousands caused to die,
Though some by wrong may live.

Who can indeed desire to see
  A premium on iniquity
From legislative halls!
  Far better losses to sustain,
Than revenues unrighteous gain
  From causing human falls,

The sin of simony was great
  When it invaded church and state,
And great its infamy;
  And shall we, in this age of light,
Pursue the wrong, ignore the right
  And reap the penalty!

THE RISING TIDE.

The temperance tide is rising,
   And wise observers say
That opponants despising
   Are sure to lose the day.

It rises in the center,
   And rises East and West;
Those who resistance venture,
   Observe and are distressed;

While others hail its coming
   As promise of the day,
When through the nation running
   'Twill sweep distress away;

When, following Maine's example,
   And Kansas, noble State,
All other States shall trample
   On what makes desolate.

THE RISING TIDE.

Ye who for this are praying,
   And working with a will,
Let there be no delaying,
   Be praying, working still.

The lives which we are living,
   Are big with destiny;
To us and others bringing,
   Or weal, or misery.

O Thou, in heaven ruling,
   Rule Thou on earth below;
The hearts of men subduing,
   Make blessings overflow.

Take Thou away the sadness,
   The bondage and the sin,
The day of peace and gladness
   Through temperance bring in;

The day so bright and glorious,
   By ancient seers foretold,
When Christ shall reign victorious
   Throughout the age of gold.

THE CAPTIVE RELEASED.

A strong and cultured man was known,
    Of rank and pedigree,
Who in his circle brightly shone,
    Respected, rich and free.

An enemy this man pursued,
    That came with stealthy tread;
By Appetite he was subdued,
    And thus was captive led.

Fast bound the alcoholic chain
    His body and his soul:
The captive struggled hard in vain,
    For self had lost control.

As when a lion in a rage
    Attempts to gain release,
But finds too strong his iron cage,
    And soon his efforts cease.

Upon his friends he calls for aid,
    Physicians try their skill;
No medicine his passion stayed,
    Or gave the power of will.

His wife and children kindly sought
    To set the captive free:
In vain affection's power was brought
    To give him liberty.

For freedom where was now the chance?
    What earthly power could save?
But he must find deliverance,
    Or fill a drunkard's grave.

More hopeless grew his family,
    And deeper his disgrace;
Reduced to abject penury
    Death stared him in the face.

To hear the truth at length he went,
    Conviction seized his soul;
But while unwilling to repent,
    He could not be made whole.

THE CAPTIVE RELEASED.

To stifle conscience hard he strove,
    Its torments would not cease;
Do what he might, wherever rove,
    In vain he sought for peace.

Then humbly on his knees he fell,
    To seek the Saviour's grace;
And soon, how wonderful to tell!
    The Saviour showed his face.

With joy he hastened to make known
    The blessing he had found,
Christ's wonderous grace and power to own,
    And spread his praise around.

As bend the lofty forest trees,
    And wave their branches high,
When blows the swiftly passing breeze
    Across the troubled sky;

So, when this preacher's voice is heard,
    The Spirit oft attends;
In many hearts the depths are stirred,
    And then their bondage ends.

SEED SOWING.

The actions of men are like seeds when sown,
From which are rank harvests of all kinds grown;
If works they do that are of useful kind,
They always are certain rich sheaves to bind;
But seeds that are worthless, or noxious, yield
A similar harvest in every field.
Most pestilent weeds, as the farmers know,
Themselves in the greatest abundance sow;
So evil will grow without care or toil,
While good, for much growth, needs a cultured soil.
The infidel sows for death and despair,
The murderer gains a rope in the air;
The drunkard, whose appetite ever grows,
For swift and eternal destruction sows!
Distillers and reckless rumsellers bold,
Are sowers indeed; and was never told
The mischief they do upon every hand,
In filling with crime and distress the land.
Move on, fleeting years, in your rapid flight,
And bring to our vision the glorious sight
Of gospel seed growing from sea to sea,
And hope fulfilled of the world's jubilee.

A TEMPERANCE SONG FOR INDEPENDENCE DAY.

Hail, honored day, to freemen dear,
   When first the stern and patriot band
Dared to assert, unmoved by fear,
   You shall be free, our injured land.

Though fierce the contest was and long,
   They hoped a better day to see,
While perseverance made them strong,
   And guided on to victory.

Here Liberty her banner rears,
   With bounteous hands her gifts she strews;
But, lo! another foe appears,
   And desolation's path pursues.

Not clad in arms he makes his way,
   But silent steals, with poisonous breath,
And thousands are his willing prey,
   Lured on to misery and death.

A TEMPERANCE SONG FOR INDEPENDENCE DAY.

And shall this foe infest our land,
   To blast its hopes, its sons enslave?
No, we behold a temperance band,
   Resolved the free-born gift to save.

Though long the war, and hard the fight,
   We onward march to victory,
And boldly battle for the right,
   Till we behold our country free.

Thou God of armies, aid bestow,
   Make us united, wise and strong;
Help us to strike the fatal blow,
   And raise the victor's joyful song.

Soon o'er our land shall proudly wave
   The shining flag of Temperance,
To show that God has come to save
   Our free and rich inheritance.

THE SUPREME REFORMER.

The Power that rules in heaven and earth,
    Performing works of might;
That gave the wide creation birth,
    And darkness turned to light;

That moved upon the shapeless void,
    A beauteous world to form,
And wise, unrivalled skill employed,
    All nature to adorn,

Still in the moral world holds sway,
    And on the night of sin
Pours light, to scatter it away,
    And day's bright beams bring in.

When wide, idolatry had spread
    Among the sons of men,
See Israel's tribes by Moses led,
    God's altars rise again.

THE SUPREME REFORMER.

How grand the work the Spirit wrought,
   When gospel heralds went,
To tell of Him who came to save,
   To lands in darkness sent!

So, when the whole of Christendom
   A moral change required,
Behold His great reformers come
   To work the change desired.

When, like a flood, the enemy
   Came in through alcohol,
An army of reformers see,
   Resolved the foe shall fall.

Thou, who can'st form, reform and guide
   The worlds that roll in space,
Our faith shall evermore abide
   In thy reforming grace.

No leagued, determined foes can stand,
   Against almighty strength;
The host which follows Thy command,
   Shall overcome at length.

STATISTICAL NOTES.

1. THE SALOON. "This saloon," "that saloon," "the other saloon," constantly figured during the *trial* of the anarchists in Chicago. Conspiritors met in saloons; dynamite was discussed in saloons, bombs were distributed over saloons; armed revolutionists were drilled above, under, or in rear of saloons; and time and time again, witnesses said, we went to such and such saloon for wine or beer. Nine-tenths of the law-breaking in the United States is hatched in saloons. This is acknowledged, but palliated by the fact that they are the headquarters for town, city, and even national elections.— *Northwestern Christian Advocate.*

2. WHAT LIQUOR COSTS. *The Toledo Blade* gives the following as the drink bill of the Nation for the year 1883:

Loss of productive labor of 700,000 drunkards, ... $175,000,000
Total cost of drinks—domestic spirits, ale, beer, etc., imported spirits, cordials, wine, etc., ... 944,629,580

Loss of productive labor of 2,138,391 moderate drinkers,	$222,392,664
Loss of time, cost of medical attendance, and medicine in sickness caused by drinking,	119,368,576
Loss of productive labor of 586,472 persons in the liquor trade,	293,236,000
Loss to employers by drinking employees,	10,000,000
Cost of supporting 83,899 defective persons, by drink, as insane, etc.,	16,779,800
Cost of supporting 59,110 paupers, etc., made such by strong drink, at $100 per year,	5,911,000
Cost of supporting 39,481 prisoners at $100 per year, made such by strong drink,	3,948,100
Loss of labor of 59,110 paupers and vagrants at $300 per year,	17,733,000
Loss of labor of 39,481 prisoners, at $300 per year,	11,844,300
Cost of police, prosecutions, court expenses, losses by juries, witnesses, etc.,	15,000,000
Value of grain destroyed to make the drinks,	33,330,396
Total	$1,869,173,416

The annual rental paid the Irish landlords is about $25,000,000. The amount paid for liquor in the same time is $60,000,000.

3. CRIME. Judge Davis, for twenty-five years on the bench of New York, declares, as the result of his judicial experience, that he has "found three-fifths of all classes of violence to be directly traceable to strong drink." A similar statement has been made by the chaplain of Massachusetts State Prison. Of twenty-nine who were committed to jail in one of the counties in Ohio, twenty-two were intemperate and four doubtful. The results in other counties were similar. Ex-convicts are often saloon keepers.

4. DISEASE. Federal statistics show that 20 per cent. of the insane in all the insane asylums of the United States went mad as the direct result of intoxicating drinks, and that 35 per cent. of the remainder were made insane indirectly by the same cause. Other countries tell a similar story: For instance, "the reports of all the asylums of England and Scotland showed that 20 per cent. of the patients were made insane by intemperance." Dr. Norman Kerr, of England, states, "At least 120,000 of our population annually lose their lives through alco-

holic excess — 40,500 dying from their own intemperance, and 79,500 from accident, violence, poverty, or disease arising from the intemperance of others." Dr. Andrew Clark, of London, says, "Out of every hundred patients that I have charge of at the London Hospital, 70 per cent. owe their ill health to alcohol."

5. POVERTY AND PAUPERISM. By a minute investigation of the pauperism of the State of New York for two years, it was ascertained that more than three-fourths of it was occasioned by intemperance, and that more than three-fourths of the ordinary tax was absorbed by the support of the poor and the administration of criminal justice. Investigations in several other States show similar results.

6. BENEFITS OF PROHIBITION. In States where prohibitory laws existed, with a population of 2,250,000, the sales of liquor dealers in one year amounted to $43,000,000. In four States, with license laws, having a population of 2,225,000, the sales amounted in the same year to $136,000,000,—more than three times as much! Of the ninety-nine counties in Iowa, under prohibition, fifty-five counties had empty jails for a whole year! In Rhode Island the number of arrests from drunkenness

decreased from 2,457 during the last six months of 1885, to 1,423 during the last six months of 1886, as a result of prohibition. The commitments to the work-house fell off fully one-half. "After six years of prohibition in Kansas, out of ninety counties, eighty-eight are free from dram-shops."

It may be taken as evidence of the good resulting from the policy of restriction, that the revenue tax on distilled spirits, for the last fiscal year, was nearly $5,000,000 less than in the preceeding year; while the statistics show that the falling off has occurred chiefly in those States where stringent restrictions upon the liquor traffic, including local option, have been adopted. The average number sent to jail in Connecticut yearly under prohibition, for five years, was 1,538. Under license, a few years later, when the population had increased only about 36 per cent., the commitments were 5,806 in a single year. The first year after the license law took effect, commitments increased 50 per cent. over the previous year in the whole State, and in New Haven County 88 per cent., though more than half the towns of Connecticut are no-license towns.

7. PROHIBITION PRACTICABLE. Not to repeat the facts already reported, which support this position, and

not to assume that any prohibitory law will enforce itself, let me call attention to what has recently been done in the State of Maine. It has been claimed that little has been done in cities by restrictive laws, from which the impracticability of doing much has been argued. Portland is a city of some thirty-five thousand inhabitants. Last year its marshal and police seized no less than fifteen hundred kegs and barrels of intoxicants in about four months. One barrel had been dug out of the earth, where it was put for concealment, the liquor being drawn out by means of a tube. Is it not evident that law is triumphing here? So, at Lewiston, nine hundred and fifty gallons of liquors were spilled on the 12th of the present month, (August, 1887) by officers at the police station, the provisions of the law, this year, being that all liquors declared forfeited shall be spilled. Near the same time, five Gardiner dealers were brought to grief, at a cost to their wallets of some $600, and over 60 gallons of liquor were secured; while similar events have taken place at Belfast, Rockland and elsewhere. It is authoritatively stated that "the sale of liquor, whether over open bars, or in secret grog shops, seems almost entirely suppressed, save in half a dozen places, like Portland, Lewiston and Bangor, where the flagrant violations of the statute are ascribed to a lax public sentiment." Effective prohibition is that which is sustained and enforced by the people who make the laws.

8. ANCIENT PROHIBITORY LAWS. The "Institutes of Menu," in India, themselves very ancient, as he says, were founded on immemorial usage. They prescribe water as the student's only beverage; direct that a man be shunned as a husband, who is a drinker of intoxicants; place the drinking of them among the vices to be avoided by the Military Class, and enumerate three varieties of fermented liquors, which the religious teacher should not touch. Both Plato and Plutarch state that prohibitory laws of a most stringent character prevailed among the ancient Greeks. Two of the twelve books of Plato's Laws are given to the history of statutes prohibiting the sale and use of intoxicating wines. Similar laws, it is said, might be traced in the histories of Chaldea and Persia; the same is also true of China and the Mahometans. The Romans had specific statutes, "which ruled first under their early kings, and later, for five hundred years, under the republic. Romulus declined to offer wine in sacred rites, and Pliny

states that Numa enacted prohibitory laws that ruled Rome for six hundred years." Thus we see that prohibition is not a new experiment in legislation, or one unsuccessful.

9. MISSIONS AND STRONG DRINK. Says Archdeacon Farrar, "Missions are incumbent on us, because we have taken with us all over the world a ruinous and clinging curse, the curse of drink. Let the shameful truth be spoken, that, mainly because of drink, our footsteps among savage races have again and again been footsteps dyed in blood. The wild tribes of America, the once flourishing Hottentots and Kaffirs, the noble Maoris of New Zealand, the native tribes of Madagascar, decimated, degraded, perishing, uplift to us in wrath and supplication their appealing, their indignant hands. We have cursed India with our drink and drunkenness, and at this moment, after so short an occupation, we are cursing Egypt too. We have poured upon these nations the vials of this plague of ours, this vice of our people, this bane and leprosy of our civilization,—are we not bound to give them the antidote? That is the only course which can avert the omen of our crimes." This argument applies also to America.

II.—Temperance in Practice.

DANGER OF MODERATE DRINKING.

Safety from intemperance
Lies in total abstinence;
Oft the gratified desire
Soon becomes a raging fire.

Tiny bushes, as you know,
Into trees majestic grow;
Little brooks the rivers form,
Sprinkling drops turn into storm.

Thus unconquered love for rum
May strong appetite become,
Subjugate the thought and will,
Madden, brutalize and kill.

Those who long this poison take
Find its powers accumulate;
Soon the wolf his teeth displays,
In the ditch his victim lays.

Appetite not gratified
Can be easily denied;
Fires that have but just begun,
May with ease be overcome.

Thousands, who by yielding fell,
Through their falling loudly tell
Drinkers moderate to stop,
And not touch another drop.

SELF-INFLICTED WOE.

Who hath sorrow? who hath woe?
Who remorse and anguish know?
By whom do contentions rise?
Who have redness of the eyes?
Who are foolish babblers found,
And unhealed have wound on wound?

Those who tarry at the wine,
Round whom evil habits twine;
Mighty on strong drink to feed,
Though they sing rude songs indeed;
Hasting in the morning light,
Following till late at night.

SELF-INFLICTED WOE.

Those who draw iniquity
With strong cords of vanity;
Who e'en call the evil good,
Light for darkness understood;
Who for sweet the bitter take,
And the sweet the bitter make!

Those have woe abundant too,
Who the baneful trade pursue,
And from selling poisonous drink
For a beverage do not shrink;
These, accumulated woe,
Retribution dire, will know.

For the havoc of the trade,
For the widows they have made,
For the poverty and sin,
Woe and crime that they bring in,
Of this mischief such the sum,
Heavy woe must surely come!

THE MURDERER AND THE VENDER.

The tragedy related in the following verses occurred in one of the towns in Maine. Of the two students referred to, one was the writer; the other is one of the Secretaries of the American Tract Society.

On coming from the grocery
　Where liquid fire was fed,
The drunkard was enraged to see
　No table for him spread.

His wife was working at the churn,
　Not ready then to leave;
She knew not when he would return,
　His supper to receive.

At once he seized an axe, to smite
　His partner to the floor!
His neighbor, having heard the fight,
　Came down and op'ed the door.

The rum-crazed man then took his life,
　By striking on the head;
He who had come to quell the strife
　Was numbered with the dead.

THE MURDERER AND THE VENDER.

Two students, teaching in the place,
  Soon after chanced to meet,
And to the grocery could trace
  The man-destroying feat.

They thought that something should be done
  To stay the fount of crime,
And casting lots, it fell on one
  To try in proper time.

He soon a pungent letter sends,
  Anonymous, but kind;
And this failed not to gain the ends
  For which it was designed.

The rumseller his trade gave o'er,
  Resolved thenceforth to be
The willing instrument no more
  Of crime and misery.

You who desire some good to do,
  May often find a chance;
By using pen or tongue you too
  May Temperance advance.

YOUTHFUL RESOLVES.

He who has made the grain to grow
    Has never made the still;
He bade the cooling waters flow
    That clouds and channels fill;
But man made whiskey, gin and rum,
That mischief infinite have done.

God made the blood to course along
    Our veins throughout their length,
He made the bones and muscles strong,
    And gave us all our strength;
By poison, man, with will perverse,
Disease creates and fills his purse.

Shall we allow such wickedness
    On us to be employed?
No, we will stand for righteousness,
    And never be decoyed;
When we to manhood's stature grow
The rum-power we will overthrow.

JUVENILE BALLAD.

Let us shun the tempting bowl;
For it takes away control,
Steals the senses, robs the purse,
Leading on from bad to worse;
We should neither touch nor taste
What brings ruin, woe, disgrace.

We have seen the drunkard reel,
Then into the gutter keel;
What a place, and what a sight!
What a despicable plight!
Let us beverages shun
By which thousands are undone.

When temptations cross our way,
May we never go astray;
Of the drunkard's fate afraid,
Let us trust in God for aid;
May He keep us from the snares
Which the tempting world prepares.

CHILDREN WARNED.

Children, now in early youth
Learn and tread the ways of truth;
Then, when later years arrive
You in wisdom's light shall thrive.

Shun the maddening saloon,
Where temptation comes so soon;
Shun the wine when it is red,
Even the taste of spirits dread.

Pleasure sparkles in the bowl,
Asking you to give control,
After comes the serpent's bite,
Would you in it take delight?

Once the habit fastened, know,
Fast to ruin you will go;
Never then the means employ
Which so certainly destroy.

TOBACCO AND REFORM.

A mean unpalatable weed
Is used a morbid taste to feed,
And tens of thousands are enslaved,
So deep the habit is engraved.

The youth who learns cigars to smoke,
Your friendly warning may evoke;
He finds his pockets robbed at length,
And habit ever gaining strength.

Some chew the weed and spit around,
Who therefore are offensive found;
The floors they stain, the stench they make
From others often patience take.

How many fill the air with smoke.
And thus their neighbors' ire provoke!
While fops go puffing through the street,
Disgusting every one they meet.

What is the profit, do you think,
Of that which is not food or drink,
But serves unnumbered slaves to bind,
Benumbs the body, clouds the minds?

A morbid appetite it feeds,
To other evil habits leads;
Gives virtue smaller chance to thrive,
And vices often keeps alive.

It serves as medicine, you say;
Sometimes, indeed, I grant it may;
It oftener serves to cause disease,
Or shorten life by slow degrees.

These greatly would themselves abuse
Who medicine when well should use:
There lurks within the sickening weed
Rank poison, on which thousands feed

Tobacco is, with opium,
The handmaid and ally of rum;
In any form their constant use
Must be intemperate abuse.

ILLUSTRATIONS IN PROSE.

1. Sir William Gull of England gave the following testimony before a committee of the House of Lords: "I mention what I saw myself in the case of one of Barclay and Perkins' draymen. The case is recorded. The man was admitted into Guy's Hospital with heart disease; he was a very stout man; he died about a quarter past ten at night, and the next day he was so distended with gas in all directions that he was quite a curious sight. Wishing to know what this gas meant, we punctured the skin in many parts and tested it. It was carbureted hydrogen, and I remember lighting on his body fifteen or sixteen gas lights at once. They continued burning until the gas was burned away." He also stated that this result of excessive beer drinking had occurred in several cases.

2. Says John B. Gough: "I pity the drunkard: he is a suffering man. His physical suffering is no light matter, but it is the smallest portion of the suffering he endures. What is that physical suffering? Did you ever see a man in *delirium tremens*, biting his tongue

until his mouth was filled with blood, the foam on his lips, the big drops on his brow? Did you ever hear him burst out in blasphemy which curdled your blood, and see him beat his face in wild fury? Is it the cramps and pains which wrench his body? No, it is *delirium tremens*, a trembling madness, the most terrible disease that can fasten its fangs on man.... Each horror is burnt into his brain, stamped upon his memory in terrible distinctness and the awful visions of the past come to mock him in his sober moments." Reader, if you would not have this terrible picture become a reality to you, shun the tempting bowl.

3. There is room for only one more illustration here. A young lady was engaged to be married. Before she gave her consent, she made the young gentleman promise that he would drink no more intoxicating liquor. They stood up before the minister to be married. He turned his face to give her his right hand, and she detected the smell of liquor in his breath. The minister said: "Wilt thou take this man to be thy wedded husband?" Looking him right in the face she said, "No!" Here was a worthy example for young ladies.

III.—Sabbatic Poems.

INSTITUTION OF THE SABBATH.

The Sabbath's grand inaugural,
   When man began his race,
And its divine original,
   Alike bespeak its place
Mid institutions formed by God's command,
   To bless the nations while the world shall stand.

Six cycles of unmeasured length
   Creation's work required;
Displaying uncreated strength,
   And wisdom much admired;
Then came the seventh, the day for Him to rest;
   This, we are told, was sanctified and blest.

In God's own image man was made,
   He therefore rest requires;
When he the Sabbath law obeys
   He such a rest desires:
Thus, in his very nature he may find
   The Sabbath for his benefit designed.

Jehovah, from amid the thundering cloud,
    In words of living light,
The ten commandments spake aloud
    On Sinai's lofty height.
And still, in tones imperative they sound
    Among the nations, all the world around.

The fourth command the Jews still binds,
    And Gentiles of all lands;
He blessedness peculiar finds
    Who keeps God's high commands;
His heart shall be bedewed with grace divine,
    The Star of Bethlehem on him shall shine.

The thirsty fields fresh showers require,
    That wilting plants may thrive;
And hungry animals desire
    The food that keeps alive:
So, after we have worked six days, we need
    The living word that will our spirits feed.

THE "QUEEN OF DAYS."

Hail, holy Day, of days the queen,
    The day when Jesus rose,
By His beloved disciples seen
    Triumphant o'er His foes.

Again upon this day He came
    To His assembled few,
Who heard His sacred lips proclaim,
    Let peace be unto you.

Thrice did He meet them on this day,
    To cheer their longing hearts;
This is the time, He seemed to say,
    When God rich grace imparts;

The day for you your Lord to meet,
    The day on Him to wait;
His praise devoutly to repeat,
    His wondrous deeds relate.

And then the Pentecostal shower
    On the disciples fell,
Endueing them with wondrous power
    For Christ to labor well.

In Patmos, on this queen of days,
    To John the Spirit came,
Who visions saw, and heard God's praise
    The heavenly hosts proclaim.

O day, of all the days the best,
    Whose light each week we view;
For thee be God the Father blest,
    The Son and Spirit too.

O never lose thy sacredness,
    Your hours we greatly prize,
Thou pledge of richer blessedness,
    Reserved above the skies.

ABOLITION OF THE SABBATH.

Abolish the Sabbath that He ordains
Who over the worlds He created reigns!
Blot out the day which was made for man,
To frustrate our Maker's purpose and plan!

Some say by their deeds: We are rulers now,
Before us must laws of the country bow;
The Sabbath we choose for a holiday,
Dissent as you will, complain as you may.

We drown Sabbath bells with railroad hum,
With blowing of bugles, with fife and drum;
Read newspapers filled with trashy news,
While worldly diversions we freely use.

On pleasure excursions we greatly rely,
Saloons and the theaters also try;
For speakers we gladly will men employ
Who would the old Sabbath day fain destroy.

How long, then, think you, can the blue laws stand,
To curb our liberty is this free land?
—Yes, truly, how long ere the house of God
Shall be by worshippers no longer trod?

ABOLITION OF THE SABBATH.

How long before crime and anarchy reign
In city and country, o'er hill and plain;
And Satan's dominion restored be found,
Where people of God had possessed the ground?

No Sabbath, no worship or fear of God,
No Spirit bestowed, no love shed abroad;
No gospel preaching, no true rest of soul,
No duty fulfilled through divine control.

The Sabbath will never annulled be known,
Till men its almighty Lord dethrone,
And they are no longer responsible
For disobeying His most holy will.

A mighty conqueror comes to reign,
To tread down the wicked and sin restrain;
And whose is the kingdom, shall all men see,
For He will lead captive captivity.

His downtrodden Sabbaths shall be restored,
His name in all lands supremely adored;
For those late in darkness *now* sing His praise,
And distant lands echo with Sabbath lays.

TRAMPLING ON THE SABBATH.

Ye legislators, will ye try
The great Law-giver to defy?
To lord it o'er the Sabbath's Lord,
That you may gain from man reward?

The Sabbath 's made for man, Christ said;
Will it serve man when it is dead?
Relax and do away its claims,
Then nothing more of it remains.

Let needless work be freely done,
Let steamboats on excursions run,
Let Sunday papers secular
Their soul-corrupting fruitage bear;

Let pleasure seekers have full swing
Dishonor on the day to bring,
Let those who work and those who play,
The Sabbath make a holiday;

Let firms and companies employ
Their power the Sabbath to destroy,
Let Church and State with folded hands
No more enforce God's high commands;

Then farewell, Sabbath's sacred rest;
Adieu, the day Jehovah blest;
Farewell, God's messages of love,
Adieu, divine, celestial Dove.

Hail, Satan's undisputed reign,
Hail, darkness, anarchy and pain;
Hail, wickedness on every hand,
And desolation o'er our land!

Pull down your pulpits, temples close;
What use for these do you suppose?
Let license rule, not liberty;
The dutiful alone are free.

Who on this earth would wish to stay
Without the blessed Sabbath day?
Restore it, Lord, and let it stand,
To fit us for a better land.

Restore it, rulers, churches too,
You both have something here to do;
Ye are God's representatives,
Through you the Sabbath dies, or lives.

PROOFS AND FACTS RELATING TO THE SABBATH.

Evidence that the Sabbath was designed for the whole race is found in Gen. ii : 1-3 ; Heb. iv : 3-5 ; Isa. lvi : 2-7; Mark ii : 27 ; Isa. lxv : 23.

That the first day of the week was designed to be the Christian Sabbath is apparent from Psalm cxviii : 22-24 ; Mark ii : 28 ; John xx : 19,22,26 and xxi : 14 ; Acts xx : 7 ; Cor. xvi : 1-2 ; Rev. i : 10.

If the seventh day of the week was desired by Christ to be observed as the Sabbath under the Christian dispensation, why did He not finish the preparatory work of redemption on that day instead of the first? He held a meeting with his disciples on the eve of the resurrection day. Why did He not meet with them during the week after this, but for the express purpose of inaugurating the Lord's Day as the Christian Sabbath? Subsequent events and records plainly show that the disciples so understood the matter, and could they have been deceived? The Jews, indeed, in general not admitting the divine authority of Christ, continued to meet in their synagogues on the seventh day. This merely gave the Apostles the opportunity to speak to them on that day ; but these were not meetings appointed by themselves. It was on the first day of the week that the meeting and celebration of the Lord's Supper recorded in the twentieth chapter of Acts occured, and that they were accustomed to meet on that day may be inferred from the regular contributions which they were required to make on every first day of the week, 1 Cor. xvi : 1-2.

Says the great Church historian Mosheim : " In the first century all Christians were unanimous in setting apart the first day of the week, on which the Saviour arose from the dead, for the solemn celebration of public worship. This pious custom, which was derived from the church at Jerusalem, was founded upon the express appointment of the Apostles, who themselves consecrated that day to the same sacred purpose; and it was observed universally, as appears from the united testimony of the most credible writers." Did this not make a change of the Sabbath in respect to the day of the week? So it seems to have been regarded, except by Judaizing Christians. And so, Ignatius, Bishop of Antioch, wrote in the year 101, shortly after the death of the Apostle John: "Let us no more Sabbatize (i. e., keep the Jewish Sabbath) but let us keep the Lord's day, the queen of days, the resurrection day."

www.ingramcontent.com/pod-product-compliance
Lightning Source LLC
Chambersburg PA
CBHW032246080426
42735CB00008B/1021